Best Wishes!

Newfoundland and Labrador

Brian C. Bursey

Published by Blue Ocean Publishing Limited, St. John's, Newfoundland, (709) 745-1908.

Printed and bound in Canada by Friesen Printers.

ISBN 1-55056-879-5

Front Cover: Kayakers explore a massive iceberg near St. John's.

Although the glaciers of east Greenland and the Canadian Arctic contribute a few of the icebergs seen in Newfoundland waters, most originate from west Greenland. Here, fingers of the 3,000 metre thick Greenland icecap reach the sea, where large sections break off through a process known as calving.

Because as much as 90 percent of an iceberg's mass is below water, their movements are determined much more by the direction of ocean currents than by the wind. Thus, most icebergs spawned by the glaciers of west Greenland travel north before moving across Baffin Bay and southward past Baffin Island. It may be several years before they are captured by the Labrador Current and swept past Labrador and the northeast coast of Newfoundland.

While the number of icebergs varies greatly from year to year, more than a thousand can be expected to pass the Island's northeast coast during the "iceberg season" of March to July. In Newfoundland waters a large iceberg is typically 10 million tonnes, with an above water height of 50 to 75 metres, while even small icebergs can measure 100,000 tonnes. Although modern navigational aids have greatly reduced the dangers which icebergs pose for shipping, they continue to destroy fishing gear, while the large waves created by disintegrating or unstable icebergs can damage small fishing vessels and onshore fishing premises.

Back Cover: West Arm, Saglek Fiord. This area of Labrador is characterized by broad U-shaped glacial valleys. The mountains in the background are over 1,000 metres high.

For Marilyn

▶   In the years before modern navigation equipment, Cape Race was the traditional point of landfall for ships travelling from northern Europe to North America. Strong winds and rough seas, aggravated by currents, thick fog and icebergs, led to numerous shipwrecks.

The first lighthouse was constructed at Cape Race in 1856, with the current lighthouse following in 1907. The lens, consisting of four optical faces, each measuring more than 2.5 metres in diameter, is one of the largest ever built. Floating on a bath of liquid mercury, it rotates every 30 seconds and, in clear weather, can be seen from a distance of 80 kilometres.

The SOS from the sinking *Titanic* was received by the Cape Race wireless station, shortly after that vessel's April, 1912 collision with an iceberg approximately 400 miles southeast of Newfoundland.

Following pages: Coastline, north of St. John's.

Fishing vessels at Ochre Pit Cove, a small fishing
village on the north side of Conception Bay. Most
such communities are referred to as "outports", a
reflection of their location "out" from St. John's.

Hand operated winches, such as this one at Adam's Cove, Conception Bay, are still used to pull fishing vessels from the water.

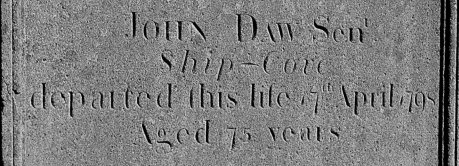

*"Time was I stood as thou dost now
and vieu'd the dead as thou dost me
ere long thou'lt be as low as I
and others stand to look at thee."*

Newfoundland and Labrador graveyards
contain many interesting headstones,
including this one in Ship Cove (Port de
Grave).

◄ A young gull seeks shelter beneath a clump of
roseroot (sedum roseum).

Historic Signal Hill overlooks the sheltered harbour at
St. John's, Newfoundland and Labrador's capital and
largest city.

Nets. St. John's has been an important
fishing centre for almost 500 years.

A fog-shrouded Signal Hill overlooks older houses
in downtown St. John's.

▶ Historic buildings rise from the waterfront.
St. John's is North America's oldest city.

The Colonial Building, completed in 1850, was home to
the Newfoundland Legislature until completion of the
Confederation Building in 1959. The building now
houses the provincial archives of Newfoundland and
Labrador.

Government House was constructed between 1827 and 1831 as a home for Newfoundland's Governors. The moat surrounding the building was intended to help protect its inhabitants from poisonous snakes, an idea which apparently originated with an English planner who confused snake-free Newfoundland with some of Britain's more tropical possessions.

Fishing vessels float in slob ice at St. John's.

▶ Cape Spear, the most easterly point in North America. Cape Spear National Historic Site preserves one of Newfoundland's earliest lighthouses, completed in 1836, as well as gun emplacements that protected the approaches to St. John's Harbour during World World II.

Death of an iceberg: In April, a large iceberg entered
the harbour at Bay Bulls, south of St. John's, where it
grounded *(left, top)*.

After three weeks the shape of the iceberg had changed
dramatically *(left, bottom)*. Wave action and melting
were contributing factors; however, the most significant
changes occurred as internal stresses caused large pieces
to break away. Abrasion by the sea floor as a result of
tides and currents contributed to further attrition.

Continuation of these processes over another three weeks
resulted in the collapse of the column on the left, and a
significant increase in the size of the arch *(above)*.
Approximately twelve hours after this picture was taken
the arch collapsed, and the fragments of the iceberg drifted
away.

Giant sunflowers attract red admiral and painted
lady butterflies.

▶ Roman Catholic Church of Saint Peter and
Paul, Bay Bulls. The gate posts are formed
by two large English cannons and two
smaller French cannons. They are
surmounted by statues of four saints
salvaged from the wreck of a ship bound
from France to Quebec.

Playful humpback whales are found throughout
Newfoundland and Labrador waters during the summer
months. Named for their unusually shaped dorsal fins,
humpbacks are five metres long and weigh two tons at
birth. Adults exceed 12 metres in length and weigh 40
tonnes. Immensely powerful, humpbacks sometimes
engage in spectacular displays, jumping clear of the
water and slapping the surface with their fins or tails.

A humpback whale rolls on its back. The characteristically white flippers can exceed four metres in length.

Archaeological site, Ferryland. One of Newfoundland's oldest and most historic communities, Ferryland was first used during the 1500s as a fishing station by the French, Spanish and Portuguese. Official English attempts at colonization began in the early seventeenth century, and Ferryland remained one of the most important centres of the English migratory fishery until the early 1800s.

The lighthouse at Ferryland Head, constructed in 1871.

European widgeon. This Eurasian duck is a regular
visitor to eastern Newfoundland.

Ring-billed gull.

Calvert. A Newfoundland dory rides on its mooring.

Castle Hill National Historic Site preserves fortifications which were originally built to protect Plaisance (now Placentia), the French capital of Newfoundland in the 17th and 18th centuries. Easy to defend, and blessed with an excellent harbour, Placentia was the centre of the French fishery in Newfoundland and served as a base for attacks against English settlements. Never captured, Placentia and other French holdings in Newfoundland were ceded to Britain by the Treaty of Utrecht of 1713.

◀ Atlantic Puffin, the provincial bird of Newfoundland and Labrador. Since puffins nest in burrows dug into soft turf, they are vulnerable to a variety of predators. Nesting on islands and coastal cliffs helps reduce this threat.

The Cape St. Mary's Bird Sanctuary is home
to thousands of gannets, murres, and kittiwakes;
as well as to the endangered harlequin duck.

Newfoundland and Labrador's largest gannet colony nests on one hundred metre high Bird Rock. Mature gannets, 70 to 80 centimetres long with a wingspan of 180 centimetres, are the Province's largest seabirds.

Erratic, Avalon Peninsula. Large boulders, such as this one perched on the side of a cliff in the Hawke Hills, are common throughout Newfoundland and Labrador. Such boulders were carried across the land, often for many miles, to be eventually deposited 'erratically' by glaciers as they melted.

◀ Eastern larch (locally known as juniper) are turned from green to gold by November frosts.

Root cellars, such as this one in Harbour Grace, kept potatoes, turnips and other root crops cool in summer, while providing protection against freezing temperatures during the winter months.

The leaves of the sundew, an insectivorous moisture loving plant, exude a sticky liquid which traps small insects.

Pink crowberries.

S.S. *Kyle*, Harbour Grace. Built in 1913, the *Kyle* served on the Port aux Basques-North Sydney run and later became a prominent feature of the coastal service between the Island of Newfoundland and Labrador. Prior to 1967, when it sustained extensive ice damage, the *Kyle* was one of the oldest steam powered vessels still in commercial service. The vessel has lain derelict at Riverhead, Harbour Grace, since that time.

▶ Harbour seals rest at the base of coastal cliffs.

◄ The historic town of Brigus, Conception Bay, was an important fishing and sealing centre during the 1800s. It was also the birthplace and home of Captain Bob Bartlett, a master mariner, sealing captain, and arctic explorer who commanded Robert Peary's ship, the *Roosevelt*, during his successful 1909 expedition to the North Pole.

English Harbour, a small fishing community in Trinity Bay.

The Harbour Grace Court House, constructed in 1830 from stone quarried on Kelly's Island, survives as the oldest public building in the Province.

◀ St. Paul's in Harbour Grace, is the oldest stone church in Newfoundland and Labrador, dating from 1835.

Horses graze in the Salmon Cove community pasture, overlooking Conception Bay.

◀ New Bonaventure, Trinity Bay. The movie *The Shipping News* and the *Random Passage* mini-series were both filmed near this small fishing community.

Called redberries in parts of Labrador, partridgeberries are a member of the cranberry family. Large quantities of the tart fruit are picked in the early fall for use in jams, sauces and baked goods.

Black crowberries are particularly common in coastal areas throughout Newfoundland and Labrador.

Dewberries. Also called the ground raspberry or hairy plumboy, this delicious berry may be found close to the ground along river banks and in other moist, sunny locations.

Happy Adventure. This outport, near Terra Nova National Park, owes its unusual name to the crew of a vessel that successfully eluded pirates by hiding in its nearly landlocked harbour during the 1700s.

Waves crash ashore near Musgrave Harbour on Newfoundland's northeast coast. Strong winds and currents, combined with exposure to the open waters of the North Atlantic, can result in 30 metre waves.

The "Mouse Hole", a natural arch south of Job's Cove, Conception Bay.

Moose. Native to Labrador, moose were not introduced to the Island until 1878. Uncertainty about the success of this initial effort led to a second introduction in 1904. A series of forest fires during the twentieth century and large cutover areas from pulpwood harvesting have created ideal feeding areas for moose, encouraging rapid dispersal and propagation. Nevertheless, moose were not reported on the Avalon Peninsula until 1941. The current population numbers about 150,000 animals.

Two varieties of caterpillar.

Salvage, Bonavista Bay. Lines and floats
are hung to dry prior to being stored at the
end of the lobster fishing season.

British Harbour, an abandoned community in Trinity Bay. Between 1954 and 1975, several hundred isolated communities were resettled by the Federal and Provincial Governments in an effort to centralize population in 'growth centres' where public services, such as transportation, schools and medical care, could be more readily provided.

Contradicting its name, the red fox occurs in a variety of colours, including yellow, brown, black and silver.

Conception Harbour.

Southern Harbour, Placentia Bay.

A red squirrel, seemingly oblivious to its thorny perch, enjoys an early morning meal of rose hips. Although native to Labrador, red squirrels were not introduced to Newfoundland until 1963. They are now common in most parts of the Province.

► Waterfall, Little Harbour River, St. Mary's Bay.

Lighthouse at Cape Bonavista, the traditional landfall of John Cabot. This lighthouse, erected in 1843, has now been restored as part of the Cape Bonavista provincial historic site. Like many early lighthouses, it once burned seal oil as a source of light.

▶ The pitcher plant, floral emblem of Newfoundland and Labrador. This unusual plant is named for its pitcher like leaves. Insects, attracted by nectar, are trapped inside by downward pointing hairs, where they eventually drown in the pool of rainwater which collects there. Nutrients from their bodies are then absorbed by the plant.

Gus, near Bonavista. Newfoundland dogs, equally at home on land or in the water, are famous for their loyalty and gentle nature.

▶ The Bonavista area contains several sites of historic interest. This locally built replica of the *Matthew* commemorates John Cabot's historic voyage from Bristol, England in 1497.

This unusual rock formation in Little
Catalina contains a third arch, not visible
in this photograph.

▶ "Naked Man", near Trinity. The term is in
surprisingly common usage for rock
pinnacles along the Newfoundland coast.

Cannon at Fort Point once guarded the entrance to Trinity Harbour.

◀ St. Paul's Anglican Church, Trinity.

Newfoundland and Labrador contains an abundance of wildflowers and mushrooms. The Burnt Cape cinquefoil *(below)* is found only on the cape for which it is named.

Right: One of several varieties of blue-eyed grass found in Newfoundland and Labrador.
Below: Northeastern rose.

Low sweet blueberry. This is the most common of several species of blueberry, bilberry, and huckleberry found in Newfoundland and Labrador. The fruit ripen in August and remain until frost.

◀ Burnside, Bonavista Bay.

Red Indian Rattle, a prominent rapid on the
Exploit's River in central Newfoundland.

Belleoram, an historic fishing community
on Newfoundland's south coast.

A spider's web glistens with early morning mist.

◄ Rhodora. This evergreen shrub flowers in June. Abundant throughout the Island of Newfoundland, it is not found in Labrador.

Pacquet. Unusually heavy arctic ice results in
a precarious mooring for this trap boat.

▶ François at dawn. This isolated south coast
fishing community cannot be reached by
road.

Wharves and stages line the shore at
Durrell, a small fishing community
on Newfoundland's northeast coast.

◀ Twillingate museum. A barking pot, once used to
soak nets in preservative, enjoys new life as a planter.

The sun sets behind a massive iceberg near Twillingate, Newfoundland.

◀ Natural arch near Little Harbour, South Twillingate Island.

A short tailed swallowtail butterfly.

Dorset soapstone quarry site, Fleur de Lys.
Over 1000 years ago, the Dorset people
carved cooking pots from soapstone cliffs
for their own use and for trade.

Above and right: Autumn frosts bring brilliant colours to birch and maple along Corner Brook Stream.

Codfish dry in the sun at Harbour Le Cou on
Newfoundland's southwest coast.

A homemade anchor, or killick. Used to moor nets or small boats, killicks are made by enclosing a long stone in a flexible frame made from alder branches or similar wood. This frame is bound at the top by twine and attached at the base to two heavier pieces of wood, known as killick claws.

The *Caribou*, one of several large passenger
and vehicle ferries connecting Newfoundland
and Nova Scotia, leaves Port aux Basques.

► Petites, an isolated fishing community on
Newfoundland's southwest coast.

Rose Blanche. The name Rose Blanche is thought
to be a corruption of the French 'roche blanche' or
white rock. There are numerous outcroppings of
white granite in the area. Stone from nearby Petites
was quarried around the turn of the century for use
in the construction of the Court House at St. John's
and in other buildings throughout Newfoundland.

This granite lighthouse, located at Rose Blanche, dates from 1873.

The Stephenville area is well known for its "blazing bogs".

◄ The setting sun produces a rare, red rainbow over Gros Morne Mountain in western Newfoundland.

Black bears, found throughout most of
Newfoundland and Labrador, are agile
climbers.

Fishermen cast for Atlantic salmon on the
Humber River.

One of several kinds of violets found in Newfoundland and Labrador.

◀ The Tablelands loom behind Bonne Bay and the community of Woody Point.

Willow ptarmigan are found throughout Newfoundland and Labrador. Their colour changes with the seasons, from mottled grey/brown in summer to snow white in winter, providing excellent camouflage.

▶ The Tablelands, Gros Morne National Park. This area owes its distinct colouration to peridotite, a rusty brown rock which is toxic to most forms of vegetation. Formed deep within the earth, peridotite was forced to the surface in western Newfoundland through the collision of the vast continental plates which make up the earth's crust. This unusual exposure was a prime reason for the designation of the Gros Morne area as a World Heritage Site by UNESCO.

The fishing community of Trout River is
located on the southwestern corner of Gros
Morne National Park.

▶ Frost turns blueberry bushes a brilliant
crimson.

The hiking trail to Western Brook Pond, Gros Morne
National Park, leads visitors past a series of small ponds
and an abundance of wildflowers.

▶ Western Brook Pond, as viewed from
its eastern end. The cliffs surrounding
this glacially carved lake are more
than 600 metres high.

Western Brook Pond. Once a true fiord, changes
in sea level following the last glacial period have
left this 13 kilometre lake well inland from the
Gulf of St. Lawrence.

The Arches, a provincially maintained public beach, is located just outside the northern boundary of Gros Morne National Park. The site features a series of unusual wave carved limestone formations.

Wreck of the S.S. *Ethie*. The passenger and freight steamer *Ethie* was wrecked on Martin's Point, south of Cow Head, on December 10, 1919. A pulley system between the ship and dry land allowed all the crew and passengers to be saved, including a baby who was brought ashore in a mailbag.

▶ The hiking trail to Green Gardens in Gros Morne National Park rewards visitors with spectacular coastal scenery, including sea stacks and sea caves.

Bakers Brook Falls, Gros Morne National Park.

▶ More than twenty members of the orchid family occur in Newfoundland and Labrador. The showy lady's slipper, shown here, is found in western Newfoundland.

Stag caribou, Long Range Mountains. Caribou are found in many parts of the province. Labrador's George River caribou herd contains an estimated 500,000 animals. Caribou start to grow their antlers in April, and shed them in late fall.

A double rainbow forms behind a marshy pond.

Above and right: In late June and early July, capelin roll onto beaches to spawn, their eggs adhering to sand and gravel until hatching about fifteen or twenty days later. Capelin are commercially harvested, and also form an important food source for a variety of other species including cod, seals and whales.

The 1000 year old Norse camp at L'Anse aux Meadows
is the only authenticated Norse site in the New World.

A red admiral butterfly rests on Canadian burnet.

Vapour from unfrozen ground has formed
elaborate frost flowers.

◀ Arctic ice crowds fishing stages at
St. Anthony Bight in early June.

Roseroot (sedum roseum), a common coastal
plant of Labrador and northern Newfoundland.

▶ Red Bay, Labrador. A whale skull rests on
the shore at Boney Beach, a remnant of
Basque whaling activity. During the 1500s,
as many as 2500 Basque whalers came to
the Red Bay area annually to hunt bowhead
and right whales.

Moravian Church, Hopedale. Close by is one of the original Moravian buildings at Hopedale, dating from 1782. For the Moravians, acceptance of a posting to Labrador represented a lifetime commitment to the furtherance of Christianity in a remote and hostile region. Few ever regained their homeland, and the sending of their children away to school in Europe represented a permanent and particularly painful parting.

◄ Lighthouse, Point Amour. This lighthouse, constructed in 1855, was just one of several built and maintained on Newfoundland and Labrador soil by the Canadian Board of Works to serve ships on the St. Lawrence route. It is the highest in Atlantic Canada at more than 38 metres.

Bakeapples. Called cloudberries elsewhere, bakeapples are found throughout Newfoundland and Labrador.

▶ Tumbled columns of basalt frame this view of Henley Harbour, Labrador.

A short-tailed weasel, or ermine, at North Arm,
Saglek Fiord, Labrador.

► Fireweed. Several varieties of this showy
plant are found in Newfoundland and
Labrador. It is common, not only to burned-
over areas, but also to roadsides, river
banks, and beaches.

Moravian Mission Station, Hebron. This large building, constructed in 1833, contained a church, classrooms, workshops, government offices, and even living quarters. Hebron is located well above the tree line, and this building, like many other Moravian structures, was of prefabricated design. Timbers and other components were cut to size in Germany and numbered prior to shipment. Hebron has been designated as a National Historic Site.

▶ Cotton grass (hare's tail), western Labrador.

Nachvak Fiord, northern Labrador.

Polar Bear. Polar bears are relatively common in northern Labrador throughout the year, and are found as far south as St. John's in spring and early summer. Strong swimmers, polar bears have been seen in open water 100 kilometres from land.

Iceberg, Labrador. Bands of sediment represent
the buildup of eroded clay and gravel on the surface
of a glacier.

▶   Heart-shaped waterfall, Saglek Fiord.

◄ Torngat Mountains, northern Labrador.

INDEX